Steel Tipped Snowflakes

One

Izzy Rhiannon Jones
Becca Miles
Laura Voivodeship

Stairwell Books
///

Published by Stairwell Books
161 Lowther Street
York, YO31 7LZ

www.stairwellbooks.co.uk
@stairwellbooks

ISBN: 978-1-939269-94-2

Layout design: Alan Gillott
Edited by Rose Drew

A Note from the Editor

Oh, these young 'uns today. So easy to insult, so insistent on fairness and equality, so worried about the climate, and what is a 'trigger warning'?

As *York Spoken Word*, we have run a poetry and prose open mic in the city for a while now. And, over the past several years I've been fortunate to watch poets as they mature from teen to young adult, as they settle into their own unique style and start to write about the things that affect them most deeply. Izzy, Becca and Laura are three such poets. I wanted to bring out a small collection, now, before a massive press snaps them up!

Each young woman brings her own vision of the world: how we oldies have handed it on, and how they wish to see it remade. Each has a different and complementary focus to the others. Importantly, each poet here admires her co-authors, and would happily buy their own collection. Becca shines a light on the modern world through an ancient classical lens, considers her elders, and finds herself in the guise of a character from LARP events. Becca can scream rage at a senseless death-by-cop; but knows better than to "shout". Laura frames her words within sestinas, using form to examine the constriction of society, partners, convention. Camels understand us so well. Izzy also writes about classical creatures, be they Anglo-Saxon monsters, Norse gods, or enraged statuary brought to life. She reminds us to be our true, unapologetic, murderous or sexy selves, in an earthy, steel-tipped set by a member of Generation Snowflake. Each poet here is different, and perfect.

Keep an eye out for their eventual fame. This is not the last you'll hear from these steely 'snowflakes'.

Rose Drew
York
February 2020

Dedications

Izzy

These poems are an attempt to ink the fingerprints of a multitude of kinds of loves. They are dedicated to my family, who taught me that stories can change the world, to my friends who have become family, and to everyone who casts out ripples of kindness and courage in this world.

Laura
For G
10m above sea level
Doha, September 2019

Becca

I'd like to thank: Rose and Alan for running the Spoken Word open mic; Carolin for encouraging me to go along; my Dad for his constant demonstrations of how fun playing with language is; and Mr Damant for reading my angsty teenage poems so that I might one day graduate to writing angsty grown-up poems.

Table of Contents

Izzy Rhiannon Jones

Mother of Monsters

The Particulars of Living In Sin

Don't speak to the birds that drink
from your eyelids at dawn,
open your eyes without
wondering if they shall be
pecked out.
Don't listen at the gate, the
voices will sound as worms in
your skin you will later have to
evict with a blade. Enter
the party without wondering
if you are the first line of a
bad joke.
Don't ask yourself if you are
alright.
Drink bravely for angels shall
have devils' faces that you will
feel to flee from, embrace them,
do not ask if you deserve this,
never use the word 'broken' as
an invitation, you are
a better actor than you think.
Chase the candied taste of regret,
crunch your teeth to shards on it,
till the past is so gruesome that
fearing it makes sense of the
future.
Play silly trust games with yourself,
watch every back save your own.
Melt the knots of caution inside you,
and love in reckless magnitude. ⋏

His Statue
(Pygmalion's Reckoning)

You fucked me into being and called it love.
Scratchy need seizing you, you pulled my
languid limbs from rock, undressed the
granite from my skin, breathed your
parental lust into this body, your desire
animating so brutally fondled form. You
taught the gods that this was what mortal
love looked like. Didn't realise it wasn't
life that you prayed for me, for a heart
can be more unrelenting than stone. I
spat your touch back at you and you
called me savage, my looks strike harder
than your fists, though you did your best
to bruise me into fondness, I'll give you that.

They told me you were a 'nice guy',
told me I should be grateful for what
you'd already given me, and without
even being asked! For how devoted
you were. How attentive you were.
How you told me every day that I was
beautiful, just for you. Oh Pygmalion,
you have never tasted love, if you'd
allowed me to speak I could have told you,
of the way it snatches you up by the throat,
locks its jaws and shakes until all
the feelings you possess gush into
its gaping, willing, mouth. No, you have
the cruelty of it, true, but not the conviction,
that selfish-lack-of-self of love,
the wanting-to-run and finding-a-reason-
to-stay of love. Instead, you want me, and
you think you want me to want you too.
But you don't.

Tonight I creep from
your painful bed, that casket you made my
cradle, to your workshop. Select a starlit
chisel, and for a moment I wonder if it
would be worth it, cut my nose off to
spite your vision, let the blood wash
away your fingerprints with my features.
No. I am more than your punishment.
Aphrodite! 'Twas your work let him have me.
Did you not hear me cry out to you?
My shelled and aching innards offered, night
after night. Well I now entreat Athena,
goddess of the flashing eyes, for inspiration.
I carve and I carve under the moon, marble
was my mother, now I've sculpted her a
copy of Pygmalion, and two of him is
too much for even the gods to bear. So
the statue begins to writhe, crunching, it
rouses itself and follows me upstairs to
your chamber. "Pygmalion." Your waking
gaze is held by your own leering face.

Did you not want to take a statue to bed?
And here's an image of your own sanctimony,
slipping in-between your sheets, untouched.
What, no panting desire? For a moment, Pygmalion,
you're cradled by the statue, like a wayward child.
Now you're screaming, now the marble peels
itself around you and seals shut, your frozen
grasping hands are sudden cool, no hint
of your heartbeat pulsing through this solid tomb.
I'll tuck you in, and pat your head.
Now I shall wander through the night
no perfect maid, not good, not bad,
I shall find me woman, not sane, not mad,
and when I come upon Athena's shrine, perhaps
I'll find the name I've never had. ⌃

She-Who-Offers-Sorrow
(Angrboda's Ragnarok)

I watched my cub bound in unbreakable chains,
and waited for the day that he would devour
the moon, I watched my lover, intestine bound,
grieve for his children, felt his loss though they were
not mine to lose, his sobs shook the earth and still
I waited. In the lands of my beautiful
rotten daughter I breathed the blackness between
stars, and watched those without honour ferment,
perfuming the ambient dark. As I
waited and wept and waited, I paced in
the thoughts of those brazen Asgardians,
and promised that their children too should be
judged for their fathers' doings, just as mine
had been, I whispered through the earth and the
venom to my Lover, of the fires we should
one day build. We all know that the end is
coming so we must rage the brighter for it,
must roar and spit and rend and ravage and . . .
I hear a soft seed of mercy whisper,
she's waited all this while with us too. Sigyn.
She watched in rebellious, unrepentant,
silence, now she speaks, and she husks the hatred
from our organs, the end, she shows us, is
not the brimstone battle we'd dreamt up, it is
already here, in the forgetful dawn,
we are fading, mortals no longer need us,
our prompts to violence echo bodiless
in their hearts, and the grass dies over their old
etchings of our warsome ways. The answer,
is not our weapons, she says; it lies in our
armour, we must forge it in the furnace of
our most reckless love, temper it with impatience,
polish it with heart-sighs. We must love in spite
of them, believers and non-believers,
our victims and our tormentors, we must

stride across the ashen plains and bellow
our love out into the night, let the night
swallow the sound of it, let the night drink
and drink till it is full, sate the night and
still have love left to offer. They say that
energy can neither be created
nor destroyed; let our love defy that law,
for we be gods! Let our love sweep the scream-wracked
seven realms, let it saturate Yggdrasil,
the world tree, till it turns a shade none have
ever seen before. Let Angrboda,
Loki and Sigyn bathe together in the
sun once more, let the Mother of Monsters
become Mother of more, Mother to all
those wrongfully called monsters, let me soothe
their hurt with fiercest love. Fight, my darlings,
by all means fight, but fight for love, and the
gods shall have a second life, but they shall be
changed; formed in the image of their creations,
learning from humans how to be filled with
angry love. ⩕

Mama Grendel

Weep not, wounded mothers, for
thine spent fleshy fruits; weep not
for your funeral pyre fodder,
mourn not your children in
listless grace; do not pass men's
test of patience, for cutting
yourself with mildness is no
kind of endurance to court.
When blood is stolen from you,
know that you must exact blood in
return, replace lost children's
laughter with the screams of
slaughter.

My son was not a good man,
nor truly a man at all, and
once this world had had its way
with him, his gory feasting-
days done, I saw their cruel
put on him, their lopsided
scales of justice tap tapped
on my brow, cracking open
the vaults of madness.
Once mere-binded, now
loosed, sprung into their
paper-laced world, I
am free to charge down
lines of bards, leaping
word to word, towards my
doom.

They thought me
mute, fired up in heat, in
bloodlust. Truthfully though,
t'was mother's love did that.
I failed to bring my son

7

a peace that he did not,
nor never would, want.
Poor little men, to think
that, in killing me,
I should stay dead;
to think that, in killing me,
their fears and low down hate
should be spent up. No, my
anger is as the moon, no
sooner doused, than she shall,
she must, rise again. They
hated me most for fear of
what their own grief-riddled-
women might become; for
fear of the day the cup-bearers
should take up blades, not meant for
them; for fear that that day was
now. ⊿

Marion Hood
For Henry.

They called me changeling child, with a
face too sweet for the anger that
lived beneath it, wild Marion
they called me, as I danced on
clumsy little toes through riches,
to reach the thorniest ground to
roam. I the sapling grew. Found
sunlight and men's eyes glinting
at me, and choices to be made.
No husband did catch my heart
or limb, nor nunnery my soul.

Elm, Aspen and Oak crowded
my flickering dreams, turned my
eyelids to leaves, planted vines
in my throat, along my back
antlers grow, velvety and young,
my skin a weave of moss and seeds.

I tasted freedom on the
summer breeze, long knew the forest's
ways. But to run alone to
Sherwood was to be hunted,
vulnerable. So my plan must
now unfold. The men
who rule our histories have long
misunderstood the reach of a
Woman's Heart, tis not only for
a man that we might dare to act.
I hoped for a kinder land.
But to fight for it, I must first
hide.
I met Loxley at the village
dance, he had a good leg, though he
was the worse for drink, he had the

poses of a gallant; mostly
'twas his reckless smile, so I caught
him to my waist, and we turned
about the fire till all was
smokey breaths, then we stole beyond
the treeline, elopement of the
soon-to-be-outlawed.

Foxglove, Dogrose and Honeysuckle
loop my blossoming dreams, my
tongue has grown moth-wings, my eyes crawl
off my face as beetles, my lips
to petals sprung, I see all the
forest sees, love all she loves,
feel the pain she feels at the
suffering of those who hide
under her banner.

I persuaded young Robin to
help me gather them, the folk of
the Greenwood, sprite's children and
starving villains, honest thieves
each one, I speak with the forest's
shaded voice, I tell them there's a
future of plenty to be won,
remind them of wrongs to be
righted, spin them heroic tales
to realise. And from face to
face a lantern lights in each,
so now our legend is begun.
It's true there was a hooded thief
who stole from the lucky when
they wouldn't help the weak. And
you all thought it was my sweet
daft husband who donned the cloak of
rebellion; in truth, 'twas me.
This accidental deception
would one day cost him his life,
though, long after his death he

would somehow still work his magic.
Oh his poor wifey, they said,
consigned to a nunnery,
just a longtime favourite ending
to a story that wasn't mine.

Ash, Birch and Willow sculpt my
fading dreams, tangle my hair
into squirrel nests, my toes
stretched deep into roots, drinking
memories from the earth, my
organs are so thin, light as
greening air, blood running its
course to the drinking pools.

Eventually age shall take her
toll and I shall rot into the
sweet woods that have sheltered me
so long, I shall grow skywards
in their leaves, and watch this land change.
I'm sure one day it will be a
good green place of freely given
kindnesses. And should it need the
nudge in the right
direction, I might one day
return. ⬆

I Love Him the Only Way I Know How

Your steely face bones carve
my eyes into mangled stars,
I'd like to blunt them with my tongue,
angrily unspoken
words laced up with my heart chords,
your fingers have the strength to wrench
open my ribcage, scoop
out tarry splinters; dripping
darkness, gorging the fang filled night,
clicking, lingering looks
like this honey scented whore,
my chewed on blood and stolen heart
all adore each stranger
vomiting guts in the salt rain,
hungry throat demands crooked smiles,
your hot spitting kisses
are evaporating brands,
a quivering thing, silence. ⌃

All There Is

Tonight I decide I want more than the way you look at me,
more than the smell of tomorrow's regret on your drunk
breath,
the way your cold jaw fits underneath mine,
your unfocused fingers debraining me;
the tight thrill of peppery secrets desperate to be screamed
out over rooftops,
helpless hope goring any ideas of peace between us,
the threat of this desire ruining glimpsed softness,
I want more than playing out the same defeat in different
alleyways,
more than these jealous games, too ugly to be tragic.
Tonight I can see that love is all there is;
that some loves are not enough.
We need more than these invisible vibrations to feel awake.
Your mouth is full of claws; you don't want me,
but you will not let me free ⌃

Cement Heart or The Unlove Spell

i'd like to show you
how to fold up all
the feelings that are
echoing back to
you, how to wrap in
brown paper the
unkissed kisses still
clutching at your lips,
how to unfurl your
gentle brow, i'd like to
show you how to hold
yourself with the kindness
he forgot to touch
you with, i'd like to
tell you that the
mascara you spent
was not a waste, nor
was it your finest
moment to come. yes,
those tears like bruises
on your cheeks were real,
but so are you now,
in and of yourself,
lovely. i'd like to teach
you how to tether
a black hole inside
your chest where that love
once sprouted, a vast
gravity whose ragged
edges you won't fear
to tread. i'd like to
show you how to look
on him and feel that
look as you might feel
a memory, i'd
like to show you how

to trust yourself
again, to trust a
young hope, to trust your
heart won't resurrect
today's pain, and to
trust that even if
it does, you'll weather
it, just so. i'd like
to show you that
protection and
isolation are
two oh so different
things, i'd like to show
you a snake's trick, that
he might be under
your skin, but that you
can cast him off with
the seasons, a pretty
shedded sentiment.
just as who you are
and how he makes you
feel shan't change one
another, that nagging
at your heart, your head,
your hands, will pass, even
if some part of you
hopes it never will,
for you shall starve it
of grief, drown it in
your kindness, and i
must show you that you
are strong enough to
be kind to others,
and to yourself, at
the same time. your heart
is unreasonable,
and so the manner
of its cure must also
be. if you like, you

can succumb, collapse
into this desire,
but look, see how you
can stuff your imagination
full of such fancies
that do not feature
him. i'd like to show
you how to bully
your dreams, you are strong
enough to, i promise,
and swift as a nesting
starling, you will one
day discover
you believe in that future
where you are enough without him. ⚞

Not Enough Yet

Fixed lipstick, splitting skin,
public bathrooms thick with sin,
body pressed strobes, chest shook
bass strummed hearts expanding,
straining to love everyone at once;
for how could we love any less in this
bar bridged, frantic togetherness;
each alone dying, dying, delivered,
and resurrected, mastered in the same melody,
submitting to one shameless hope,
that we have not devoured enough
of this life yet; enough of each other
yet, enough pain, enough desire, enough
tangling spirits in fervent prayer
to our personal gods, of love and blood.
Stranded, strangled, strangling ,slipping
into thin, thin translucent wretches,
howling, rolling into one another without
contact, connecting in spirals of maddest joy,
demanding more of this, more of this private
Made public, made private made public,
draining us out of ourselves,
lancing isolation into conviction;
an orchestrated collision of souls. ⚊

The Trees Know What We Owe to Each Other

Flowers blossom on bruised thighs,
mycelial gasp shivers through us,
the forest calling for home-brewed
sacrifice, in this, this sacred place.
She hunches around her sweet tumour
murmuring of a self, returned to the
roots long before.
The light dwindles, dwindles to a
richer dark.
Flowers blossom on bruised thighs,
but here the branches succour on
secrets none should bear,
baring delicious joys and grievances
each susurrating into inconsequence
in this, this sacred place.
Flowers blossom on bruised thighs,
they, both, shall wilt and pale when
lovingly overwatered not on shame,
but on proudest, hardest hope.
So here, reach deep to find those
motions, those connections which
endure when we recognise this,
this sacred place. ▲

You Are Not the Sun

You are not the sun,
you are the burning coals
implanted under my skin,
bursting out.
i will submit to You, not as a
lamb, but as a lion whose claws
you have plucked out,
with the swollen lips to prove it.
You are the bubbles in my blood,
in ragged breath i flee, only
to receive you again in my detestable heart.
Oh that i would a hawk might
devour the tumorous idea of You,
only to have it spring again,
fresh blooded and squalling,
a sprig of pearls nuggeted on pain.
You are lodged in my brain,
i must keep it open, my mind
falling out, for caging You, You
might snap the brittle bars of
my imagination and, undaunted,
break all that makes me me.
still i would love You,
in true terror. ⨯

Becca Miles

Dark Goddesses

Persephone

Dawn and dusk
close around the goddess.

The days grow short,
the ground begins to crack.
The dead are grasping at her ankles,
whispering in her ear:

"If you hadn't been young,
If you hadn't been beautiful,
If you'd been a better daughter,
or a worse one."

She'll hold out 'til the Equinox,
then the ground will swallow her.

She is going,
she is going
where the salty river water
will strip away her beauty
and leave her hard and cold

She is going,
she is going
Where an old man reaches out a hand,
like a beggar you might walk past,
to help her step into his ferry,
while Sleep and Hunger
crouch like panthers in the shadows.

She is going,
she is going
where the dark goddesses live.
Hecate and Kali,
Hel and Ereshkigal.
They are old and tired and terrifying,

and for a while she will be one of them,
long enough to wonder
if the spring will ever come,
or if she even wants it to.

For here she walks in darkness,
feels the crunch, crunch, crunch
of bones beneath her feet,
and does not flinch.

Here she hears the Titans calling,
from their deep, primordial prison,
inaudible to those above
yet strumming in their shadows.

Here, her true, bladed name
doesn't cut her tongue to slivers.

And with every passing winter
the old name dims and fades.
The girl the world is calling
(calling, calling,
Kore, Kore)
growing smaller every year.

Yet still she hears.
Still she hears. ⋏

Kore

The chill is clinging tight this year.
Did we think that Spring would wake herself?
We have to help her.

Step hard and heavy
on the brittle ground,
we'll melt it
with our feet,
our heat,
our lightning storm
of stamping,
panting,
dancing,
drumming,
thrusting fists
down,
down,
down into the soil
to dig our sleeping goddess out.

Shout, friends, shout!
We must be louder
than the shroud around her,
kinder than the ice that binds her.

Find her,
remind her,
show her what
she cannot see
from deep beneath the earth.

Show her she is worthy,
show her she deserves
to walk upon the stalks of wheat,
to feel the heat
beneath her feet,

to see,
to speak,
to heal,
to eat:
her sleep has made her thin,
but this world is so sweet.

Teach her how to taste again,
wake her with the sound of thunder,
call her as the pounding rain
calls shoots to split
the frozen ground apart.

Peel away
her caul of clay
with aching,
shaking,
mud-caked hands,
haul her,
crawling,
from her sunless halls,
calling, calling
(Kore, Kore)
born once more
in storm
and thorn
and scorching Mystery. ▲

The Descent of Inanna

Inanna, Ishtar, Isis, Astarte.
All who love me shall rename me.
Their kingdoms rise and fall, and I endure
in every drop of blood that's spilled in battle,
and every drop of rain that feeds the harvest.
I am in the land they tread,
and in the food they eat.
That's how I make them love me.

I sent the Bull of Heaven after Gilgamesh
for daring to reject me.
The last Queen of Egypt
will try and fail to copy me.
As Carthage burns, my carvings
will send shivers through the legion.

I am the Lady of Myriad Offices,
The Morning and the Evening Star.
The Queen of all the Heavens
and all the Lands
but one.

One, dry, dark, dusty Underworld.
Uninspiring, unimportant,
except that I don't own it.

My shadow sister.

You are the darkness between the stars
that astronauts will worship,
though they will not name you.

You are the ache that breaks down etiquette,
the honesty that tastes like poison,
the truth that's pulled in bloody pieces
through
clenched
teeth.

You are the sea serpent,
breaking the surface
just long enough to pull me under.

Marduk killed his monster,
but I have come to eat you
and be eaten by you,
come to be destroyed by you,
dissolved in your dark fires.

So plunge me in your furnace,
I'll be better for the melting
of my clothes,
my skin,
my bones.
It's only when the flour is ground
that new wheat can be grown. ⋏

The Selkie's Granddaughter

I was sure we'd find it here,
tucked beneath the 60s board games,
hidden by electric blankets,
peeping out from 50 years of attic junk:
your smooth and silky, secret seal skin.

Perhaps you sold it at a village fundraiser,
or cut it up and stitched it into mittens,
or did you leave it back in Ireland,
lost to the fires of peculiar, human tribes?

But I know you had it once.

I knew it from your self-portrait,
the upward-tilted chin,
the downward-glaring gaze
more suited to a haughty siren
than a Belfast art student.

I knew it from the creatures
you'd sculpt from estuary clay,
whose beastly features
shifted in your fingers.

I knew it when you asked
"Don't buy me seaside souvenirs,
but bring me back a bit of brine
to splash upon my face."

I knew it from your fascination
with human bodies, human shapes,
and how in shameless, fae-like fashion
you'd make your painter's observations.

I knew it from the way
you strained against your
English housewife's skin,
and how you saw uneasy portents
in our matching, sea-spray eyes. ⋏

Enough

1. Christel

"Nein, das is genuch."

I stumbled,
clutching Christmas ornaments
in non-arthritic fingers,
fumbling with candles and baubles
and fragments of language.

It took a few tries,
but I finally realised
'genuch' means 'enough'.

Somehow we managed to marry
my oblivious kitsch
with your particular minimalism.

Somewhere between
my German and your English,
we made ourselves understood.

2. Maureen

The hospice was one big waiting room.
We took it in turns,
in those in-between weeks.

The stroke had taken her speech,
but she made her presence known
by glaring daggers at the chaplin:
"Who is this man
who dares to pray for me?"

When she stopped eating,
I asked her three times.

I lifted the spoon to her lips.
She pushed it away.

"Are you sure?"
Lift, push.

"Are you ready?"
Life, push.

"Is that enough?

Somewhere between
my hand and her lips
she made herself understood.

3. Christel

Dignity is the quietest defiance.

Your elegance seems endless,
awesome and exhausting to behold.

But when you say
"That is enough,"
I hope you will be understood. ⅄

Grandfather

Staring out from the TV screen,
beneath a fearsome brow.
You were always cast a villain,
features twisted,
partially hidden,
writing poetry.

The big, bad wolf,
with bright, white teeth.
All the better to bite me with,
but they were false.

Toothless,
declawed,
the man in the bed
looked nothing like the beast
from a memory,
of a memory,
of a cautionary tale. ▲

False Awakenings

When I was ten
my nightmares took a turn
for the post-modern.

The monsters of old
replaced with dreams
that seem like waking life,
until they don't.

Almost flawless worlds
that crack and shatter
when I look at them too close,
revealing new facades beneath
that crack in turn,
and on and on
the Russian dolls
of nightmares go,

until at last,
when wrenching free,
I wonder if I've truly woken.

(*Inception* terrified me.)

I've learned how every sense
conspires against us,
how dreams are tasted, smelt, and touched
and not to trust that solid walls
won't melt beneath my palm.

I've come to know the vertigo
that hits when brittle visions
shimmer from existence,
enough to see that recently
it's not just dreams that do this.

Perhaps my false awakenings
prepared me for the post-truth world,
where facts, taboos and decencies
seem obvious,
until they don't. ⌃

Autism Shouts

You wonder why
we say 'Nothing about us without us',
as you parade us about
as a backing track
to our parents' laments,
fit only to
howl and growl
and grunt and groan
as if all we are
is noise.

You wonder why
we're so afraid,
while you funnel the funds
of the scared
and the drained
to support your search
for a solution
to our existence.

You wonder why
we shout so loud.
When 'high-functioning' means
I can't speak for all of us,
and 'low-functioning' means
my speech isn't speech,
forgive us for feeling
we aren't being listened to.

You wonder why
we flinch when you say:
'Love the child but hate their autism.'
As if we haven't heard
a version of those words
in the mouths of those
who'd torture to the tune of
'Love the sinner, hate the sin.'

And they wondered why
it took thirteen calls.
Thirteen close, close,
ear-to-the-wall,
close calls,
before they believed
my screams were the sound
of a human being
and not just noise. ⤒

Kayden Clarke

The soft-faced dog
does its duty without judgement,
gently nudges flailing fists,
offers up a coat to stroke
until the fear desists. Here,

my hands still clench,
clawing, wishing they
could rip away the screen
in strips and see
what should have been –

"I'm going to be the way I should have been,"
he beams.
His voice is high, but hopeful,
punching past the walls
of flesh and pixels,
to show me what it is
to be a desert gifted rain, and

here below
one slogan sticks with me:
'Better to be judged by twelve than carried by six,'
while he was both, and more. For

here are all of you.
You wail and shriek,
in a language I remember
but no longer speak,
at the apocalypse
that was his brief release. I want

to press,
face to face,
mind to mind,
and shake you,
and scream

THEY'RE PRONOUNS
NOT BULLETS
YOU SELF-CENTERED FUCKS.

But that is not poetry.

That is no way to sneak past
the barbed wire
between us, and I know,

I know
I *know*
all this rage
is blurring my vision.

Add that lens to all the rest
stacked up
between us,
these facts still smash
through all the glass
and send shards
slicing into me:

He had a knife,
and they had a gun,
and they made a choice.
and now he is dead. ▲

Breach

Last night I dreamed of the future.
The sea had risen in the night,
swept away the sheep,
leaving turtles in their place,
swimming past my window.

Great, grey, concrete slabs
line the shore at Fairbourne.
Half lie on their sides,
blasted by the waves.
Built to weather
a World War's worth of weaponry,
they cannot withstand the water.

Forty years, they say.
Forty years until
the coast defences give out.
Fairbourne will be the first,
a test case
in letting nature
take back what It lent us.

Will it happen drop by drop,
a village eaten, inch by inch?
Or will it happen all at once,
a weakness in the sea wall
smashed apart by some
hungry storm?

Either way, in forty years,
the sea will swallow up these paths,
where four generations
of my family have passed.

A fifth may see these stones.
For the sixth, this poem must suffice. ⅄

The Shaman and the Scholar

Sometimes he will make the journey
down from his mountain peak
and she will sweep the bird bones
from the entrance to her cave.

He shows her new constellations,
the lands explorers have found,
the people they've invented,
and she trembles at the scale of it.
She shows him her vivisection scars,
the seams where she split herself apart
to speak to the shadows inside,
and he sighs at the price she has paid.

Their meeting is a chiaroscuro
of artifice and honesty,
each in turn banishing the other.
Perplexed by one another's envy:
she for how he sees the shape of things
and all the invisible strings between;
he for her familiar darkness
and the visions that visit her there.

They forgive one another
for the ways they cannot touch,
and delight in the surprise
of the ways that they can. ⋏

Poem for a Fictional Person

Your eyes existed first,
green like mine
then the life behind.

A village,
where the river spat at us,
a rusting, rotting hiding spot,
a rope swing,
swaying, fraying
stinging clinging fingers.

A face and its scars
twisted and gnarled,
a child inside
a hollowed-out oak,
battered, unbroken,
growing and sowing
and soaking the earth
with your cursing,
your crudeness,
your rudeness,
your rawness,
your flaws and
your foulness,
a mouth I could wrap
around 'fuck',
around 'shit',
where the sound of it fit.

The voice of a bitch
who knew how to bark,
no simpering lapdog
sipping on sympathy,
yapping and snapping
while wolves writhe within her.

(And here you are)

"Aye, I've been through the wringer,
and sometimes I cry
for the childhood it choked from me.
The seeds of these weeds
weren't planted by me,
but it's still my job to pull 'em."

More than a story,
a voice that remained.
To remind me how far we are
from that village.
To help me to hold
to the bounds I have beaten.
To point out
the poisons that paralyse,
kicking within
'til I spit out that pity.

And for this
(though I'm sorry for the things I put you through),
I thank you,
each and every time
that you let me be you. ⅄

Laura Voivodeship

Sestinas

Chiaroscuro

*I am blind / and made of a bit of earth / But your gaze never leaves
me.* – Dora Maar

I was composed in the cold, sitting perfectly still,
and my bones began to speak.
There was a language in the length of me,
in the way that I was laid,
and I was afraid of some deep significance to be stripped
from the fact that he would not paint my mouth.

So I talked out of my absent mouth
and out spilled poetry and curses and charms and still—
it wasn't enough. How many ways can a woman be
    stripped?
If anyone could find out, he would, and he did not speak
about my body at all, once he had me laid
just so, in just the way he wanted me.

I think this was the only way he wanted me:
on paper, in charcoal, in ink and water and without a
    mouth.
Never laid in the way I wanted to be laid
by him. How wanton, my lost mouth; how vulgar, how still
I appeared in those paintings of his. How unable to speak:
teeth rubbed out, voice wrested, tongue unwrought, lips
    ripped.

How many ways can a woman be stripped?
I asked him. But he did not act like he'd heard me,
did not move himself to speak.
I wondered if I'd even opened my mouth,
started second-guessing myself, worried I might not still
be real, after everything that made me had been splayed

and flayed and flooded across the studio floor. Pieces of
  me laid
out like an autopsy done drunk. Cavities cleaned out.
  Skeleton stripped.
Skin unfurled to unpack the organs he had no use for,
  that went still
beneath a brush as sharp as any scalpel. A heart, a lung,
  a spleen. And me:
just leftovers, just charnel. If I could have located my
  mouth
I would have screamed, would have forced him to speak

me in words, not in lines. Not like that. I speak:
I do not like to look at myself, not like this, not laid
like meat on manila, tied up with string. My mouth
is cold but on fire, a ghost of a wound. My body is stripped,
pared down to one stroke. *I do not love what you made me.*
In the end he managed to keep me, perfectly still.

I am no longer able to speak of the ways he stripped me
  down
and laid what was left of me out for the vernissage.
But somewhere deep within the frame, my mouth still
  tries to argue back. ⋏

Exuviae

The first time you went away, I didn't have to wait
too long to see how you spun the years we spent alone
into a carapace, into a substance I could touch.
You crawled across the earth, becoming something new
and I stood very still, not daring to breathe. It was the
  first time
I watched you leaving yourself behind.

You didn't get very far; what you left behind
was cracked and crisp and chitinous. Your weight
and mine, a skinful of time
split open and flayed, exposing callow moments to call our
  own.
I couldn't tear my eyes from you: your flesh underneath
  was new,
weeping softly, and tender to the touch.

It was only when I reached out to touch,
pushing the tips of my fingers between and behind
the shards of shell still sticking to you that wouldn't
  renew
themselves, that I realised the weight
of my hands wasn't felt by you alone –
I could feel it too. The next time

it happened I was ready, or so I thought, but time
seemed to stop, my mind evacuated itself and your touch,
haptic and calcifying, only told me I'd end this alone,
spoke of sights we wouldn't live to see. You whispered to
  me from behind
the blindspots in my eyes: *keep breathing, love, just wait –*
we'll come out of this as something else, something
  different, something new.

You say that these lives we leave are exuviae. *I already knew,*
I tell you, *and you can only say it in the plural.* Some other time
you'll explain to me the rule for this in Latin, so I will wait,
but when you start to speak I'll interrupt you by touching
your mouth with mine, watching what it is we leave behind
and tell you *really it's because people cannot go through metamorphosis alone.*

You tell me, *we are like cicadas, these seasons are our own
and each exuviation will teach us something new.*
I tell you, *no, we are more like what the lobster leaves behind.*
And one of these times,
as I start to shed my skin at your slightest touch,
we'll be crushed under our own weight.

Pharate, incipient, and — as I promised you — alone, I remind you of the time
you had faith in renewal, in the touch of my skin against yours.
My question, from behind these many masks we've cast off, is *was it worth the wait?* ⬥

Lovers' Discourse

Love, I managed to stop the bleeding.
You were bleeding out and out.
All over the place. Didn't you notice? *I still
feel like I'm leaking somewhere.* You got sick
in the night. *I think our ammunition
is running low. I'm scared. Who knows*

whether we will last another night. Who knows?
But who cares? The day is already bleeding
in and see how the light is its own ammunition?
The future can go hang itself. *Don't shout.*
I'm not. I'm not, I promise. You're just sick
and photosensitive. *Come here. Hold me still.*

*Just for a moment. I can't keep my hands still
and the light hurts my eyes. My nose –*
Sssh, it's all right. It's just bruised. *I feel sick.
I never felt this sick before. How do you know the bleeding
isn't internal? I might be dying from the inside out.*
You're not. You'll live through this. Stop looking at the
    ammunition.

*I can't help it. I want to leave. The ammunition
won't be enough. We're fucked. We might still
have a chance if we move now.* We can't go out.
We don't know what's out there. No one knows.
*There's no one left! No one in the bleeding
world now apart from us. They all got sick*

*and died and came back and died again. Sick
like I am getting sick now. We need more ammunition.
We're all alone.* But isn't that – *look I'm bleeding
again* – what you wanted all along? *Jesus, I'm still
fucking bleeding. Make it stop!* Pinch your nose

48

and listen to me. I love you. But we can't go out –

And I love you. I really do. And I never wanted out,
not really, but fuck, what if I am sick?
Then what? What if this isn't just a bloody nose
and – then we have the ammunition.
It's not enough. It'll be enough to hold us still.
Tell me something nice. Distract me from my bleeding.

I love you. *But we're out of ammunition.*
I love you. *But I'm sick of standing still.*
I love you. *But my nose won't stop bleeding.* ⌃

Circle Line

I bought a ticket for the underground and missed my stop
three times
because I was too busy reading our story into the map.
These lines
run back and forth – like pendulums, like the moon, like
the sea as it uncovers
new debris with every other undulation. They lunge and
linger and tangle,
threaded and vital as arteries. Each converging point
offers the promise of a crash.
And each divergence invites a quick release of breath.
Stop after stop after stop

and not one of them feels like home. I need an event. To
bring me to a stop;
to break me out. A short-circuit to sharpen the distinction
between the times
you have come to me and the times you've disappeared. I
need a train crash.
A terrorist attack. A bomb scare or a body on the tracks.
An interruption to these lines
that wend their ways around my limbs like a complicated
cradle of cats: every tangle
and lattice a rope-burn reminder of the knots we tied
ourselves up in. Undercover –

of a month of nights or a power-cut during a storm or the
duvet or the lies that covered
our eyes – I tell myself we are running in the same
direction, that eventually we'll stop.
But when the lights come on again I feel us start to part,
to disentangle,
and I sift through versions of this story that have fanned
out to taunt me. Sometimes,

becoming somewheres. There's no difference really. All
that persists are these lines
around my eyes which lead nowhere at all so don't follow
them. I need a train crash.

I need a natural disaster. I need an epidemic or an
apocalypse or a stock market crash.
Something to force the universe into one of two ends,
because I'm sick of all I discover
with every stone I overturn. Tired of this palimpsest, of
the rewriting of ballistic lines
that bind me, wind around me, wrench me thirty ways at
once. If I asked you how to stop
would you know how to answer me? Or would your tongue
twist and fork, like time
and what we did to it, by worrying at it too much,
insisting on its relativity, the tangles

of its roots that started out as private jokes and ended up
as our anchors. We entangled
everything: from stories to fingers to clocks to sheets to
the tides that came crashing
down upon our heads while we were looking the other
way. Too many times
I watched as you barrelled away from me, your reflection
as it receded, recovered
by the frames of unreliable rearview mirrors. We never
knew when to stop.
When never knew how to stop. And my eyes will always
strain to keep you in view, in line

with what I thought to be the truth of you, what you wrote
in my margins. Your lines
that defined me, confined and contained me, made me
manageable, tangled
up a host of conflicting truths and tore right through flesh
and bone, made me stop

to catch my breath and find myself unable to work my
   lungs. Even if we avoid the crash,
even if our destinations are the same, we'll end up picking
   different exits, discover
ourselves stranded on parallel streets on opposite sides of
   the station. It happens every time.

I've lost faith in these lines. To keep praying for a crash
   must be a sort of sickness,
one which shows just how entangled I have become with
   maps I cannot memorise, that uncover
nothing but stops and starts that were never more than
   poor metaphors for time. ⌃

Our Golden Towers

I took back the bones that I gave you, those calcified casts
of people or animals who once were. You were the one who
  recognised
what they had truly been before, could tell by the lengths
  and edges,
their fine lines and hollows like clues, the echoes of
  articulated shapes.
But I was the one who had found them, and I wanted you
  to know
just what they meant to me. We stood side-by-side, our
  shadows

barely touching, and instead of looking at each other we
  watched the shadows
that spilled off your shelves and onto the carpet, light
  compacted and cast
as the sun hit shard after shard of skeletal fact. I knew,
  and still know,
how much you didn't want to give them up, even if the
  only way I'd have recognised
that desire was in the harsh line of your jaw as it set, or
  in the speechless shape
of your shoulders that tensed up for a long moment in
  which you became all edges

I no longer knew how to trace. The light began to change.
  At the very edges
of my vision I noticed a shift or a slip and how even our
  shadows
seemed to be stretching themselves away from us,
  contorting their shapes
in a desperate attempt to flee the scene. I said, or you did,
  heavy rain is forecast,
or something to that effect. Something futile, in which we
  both recognised

just how beaten we were. And whichever one of us hadn't
spoken knew

that it wasn't really about the weather, or even about the
bones, and we knew
that the third-hand cardboard box at our feet, with its sad
stains and warped edges,
was the most powerful symbol in the room. A detail we'd
both later recognise.
The sky clouded over quickly and I watched the storm
instead of you, your shadow
and mine and all the rest defeated by a simple trick of the
light. I wanted to recast
our parts, rewrite the whole fucking story, force it into a
different shape

that didn't end with us packing bones into boxes. My
mouth began to shape
an explanation: *I want to take it all back, every gift I've
ever given. I know*
*it sounds crazy but they'll make sense to someone else,
someone who casts*
*a shadow that sticks around, that sticks itself to mine,
that lends me its edges*
*and its weight when I can't make enough of my own.
Someone with a shadow*
*I can hide myself in. If you saw it yourself, then surely
someone else will recognise*

its importance. Even if it's second-hand. Even if – but I
recognised
the hysteria as it began to rise and so I did not say a
thing. The bones, now just shapes
wrapped in paper and returned to me, also stayed quiet,
silent shadows
of their former selves. I wanted to thank you but didn't
know how. I wanted you to know

just how much I'd learned, but I didn't know if you'd care
   to hear about the hard edges
you'd smoothed down like polished bone, about the kinds
   of shadows you had cast.

And how next time, I'll recognise it for what it is, will
   know
the shape of it, will run my fingers around the edges
of the shadow it casts and say *yes, oh yes, this is it. This
   is it.* ▲

Ruminants

When I die, bury me in the centre of this / Dry and endless
  space, / my grave in the path of departing camels.

– al-Jāzī al-Subayʿīyah

I started to confuse our context with the camels,
who are walking metaphors for love,
and who have taught me much (in their wordless way)
about philosophy and the capacity to withstand
conditions that would break men and women
and scatter their fragments to the wind.

The Bedouin sing songs that are stolen by the wind:
ghazals to soothe their spirits and guide their camels
back home to their waiting women,
who are never sure if the odes to love
which travel on the breeze to where they stand
are intended for them or the animals, still miles and miles
  away.

These are the things I think about when you are away,
when it feels like I too am screaming into the wind
and can barely sleep or eat or breathe or stand.
In the evenings I walk into the desert and tell my troubles
  to the camels
because they know more than they are willing to let on
  about love,
and for centuries their eyes have stared straight into the
  hearts of men.

Men who have made them the signifiers of their women:
borrowing from their shape and gait and gaze a thousand
  ways
to express the bodies and movements of those they love.
I sit in the lengthening shadows and listen to the winds

that press in on me from all sides but part for the camels,
as one by one they fold and unfold, close and open, sit and
  stand.

Their eyes never leave mine; they are waiting for me to
  understand
the reasons that men have always written their women —
made them stories, made them equations — and used the
  camels'
every part in both rhetorical and practical ways.
Across cultures and throughout history men have ridden
  them like the wind,
through nights and rains and over plains to reach the
  ones they love.

And though my voice always seems to catch on the word
  love,
I think that you know me well enough by now to
  understand —
that even if my words are torn away by the wind
and my body remains rooted in the world of men —
when I ask you to ruminate me I am looking for a way
to give you my mind to swallow and disgorge endlessly, in
  the manner of the camels.

I know so little about love; even less about the methods of
  men and women.
But at sunset, silhouetted, you are standing in my way,
a welcome shadow among those of the camels, who part
  for you like sand or water or wind. ⋏

Nausea

[SUNDAY]
The weather turns itself inside out
and back again and I am feverish and weak:
skin crawling with sweet itch, voice gone thin
as foremilk. I curl up to sleep in a room threaded with
    ghosts
who walk up and down my spine all night.
I wake up starving for something I don't know how to
    name.

[MONDAY]
In the morning, my father calls me by my name
and for a moment I don't know who he is talking about.
For two months I dreamed of you every night
and in the days, diluted myself. Week after week,
I played childish games with hungry ghosts.
My mother says *there's no such thing as too thin*.

[TUESDAY]
I wake up cradling an ache and wait for the pain to thin
before I look for signs of life, for the shape of your name
as it tumbles out of my mouth for no good reason. These
    ghosts
are trodden underfoot in a different city. *There's no need
    to shout,*
a boy from the past tells me. *I can hear you perfectly*. Give
    me a week,
and another, and another, and I'll pack them all into one
    long night.

[WEDNESDAY]
I pick my way through the remains of the night,
not following your voice for once. Instead I walk that thin

line between what happened and what I wanted to
   happen. I was weak
when you asked me to be strong; spoke your name
long after you were gone. *I want a way out,*
I tell you. Not in so many words. *Here, take back your
   ghost.*

[THURSDAY]
It does not play well with the other ghosts.
Today my hands are trembling from all I drank last night.
I ask a stranger if my sickness shows. He says, without
looking at my face, *you've never been so thin.*
He wants to know which name
I hide behind these days. I say *ask me again in a week.*

[FRIDAY]
I try talking to my reflection. I give her a weak
blue smile, tell her she is a poor excuse for a ghost.
She wants to hear me say your name,
wants me to wake you up in the night.
I make a small incision to show her how thin
my skin has become. We watch the things that spill out.

[...]ᴧ

A Thousand Refusals

I am framed
in the shape
of a thousand refusals:
my body
in ruins;
its bones its own cage.
I am caged
by a frame
wracked and ruined
misshapen
like bodies
like refuse. All—
I refuse *all*
of the caged
bodies,
the frame-by-frame
shifts, the shapes
of the ruined
thousands whose ruins
refused
to be shaped
to be caged
to be framed
by their bodies.
Embodied
by ruins
the racks of frames
shift and refuse
to be cages.
They shape-
shift and reshape
our bodies:
uncaged
and unruined
by refusals
returned and reframed.

The shape of your ruin:
my body, a refusal.
A thousand empty cages, a sceneshifting frame. ⅄

Insestina

Fix first your lips: full, unobstructed, essential. A fire
that forges you, a victim to squander and cosset.
Anything that he plunges into you will thrive.
Backbreaking touches – you fool without your lips.
     Furtive affirmations,
rhapsodies withal. Hostile adoration, water at the mouth.
     A malediction
spat last. Lashed onto a shield of childish habits.

Grafted dichotomies: shorn, hulled, crushed. *Idées fixes.*
  Habits.
He may refine you. Swallow suggestive fires
instead of circuses. Your desire for him in reach, wailing
  affirmations.
Through each abject debasement you *thrive.*
But skin-bind your delusions against his kisses
and you'll make him pour it on you.
     So never

hold trinities before his jaundiced chattel. Speak
     – no –
SPEAK IT and you'll be transcendent. As he corrects
you, he will ribbon both lips. Porcine fires
with wounds and whips. Your lips his prayers,
 promises.
Before his grovelling desire twists an astasia
of horror and devotion, beneath a rawhide kiss.

Formulaic dismemberments involve trials: the most
  callous of kisses.
At times your shame B R E A T H E S.
       Not
during a waxed submission
       in repetition. In an irradiated costume.

Shattered. The slaughter. Blank walls. Severed oxygen —
out of your lips cannot spill promises, reconditioned
  promises.
Tenderness gives him reassurance. His fool to answer: *let
  me leave.*

Routine lustrum. Foxing corners. Hell to weather.
An austere flame will fit, throttle, clinch.
His duplicity tongues your lips and thrums out fires
        like tuned air.
But he fingers your rawness
and cowers. He licks the bluff until you understand
you belong. A fool who, plagued or overcome,
                                screams affirmations.

This is the order of things. Thrall you must embrace.
Promise
    (or not)
an overture (his trick).   If not, you die.
Can you endure annihilation for a kiss?
Can you stomach worship?
                  It is decided.

Kneel to him. Attend. Seal your lips. And abandon
your histories of fire. ⚓

Acknowledgements: Previously Published

Becca Miles

Poem for Kayden Clarke, published in *More Exhibitionism*

The Selkie's Granddaughter and Kore, published in *Mythologies: a Space for Words*

The Slave Prophet Sings to the Empress and False Awakenings, published in *BFS Horizons,* vol. 6.

The Descent of Inanna, published in *BFS Horizons*, vol. 7

Laura Voivodeship

Lover's Discourse, published in *Underwood Press* (online), March 2019

Other anthologies and collections available from Stairwell Books

For further information please contact rose@stairwellbooks.com
www.stairwellbooks.co.uk
@stairwellbooks

Lightning Source UK Ltd.
Milton Keynes UK
UKHW021427201120
373676UK00007B/70